Where Are the Hamsters?
By Emily Howard

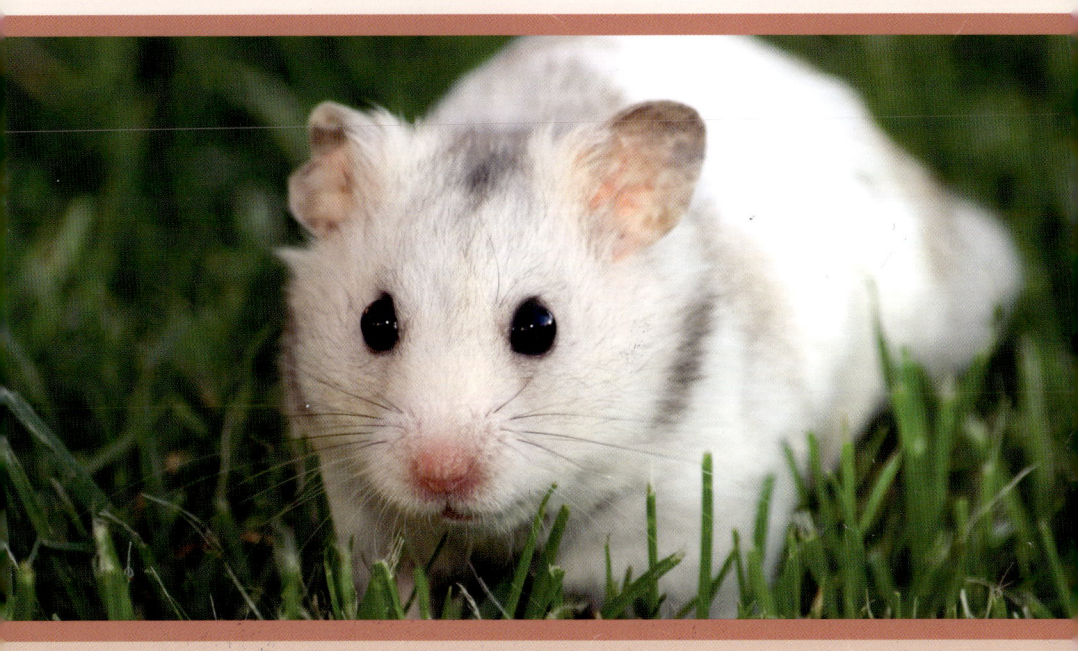

Pioneer Valley Educational Press, Inc.

Look in the cup.

3

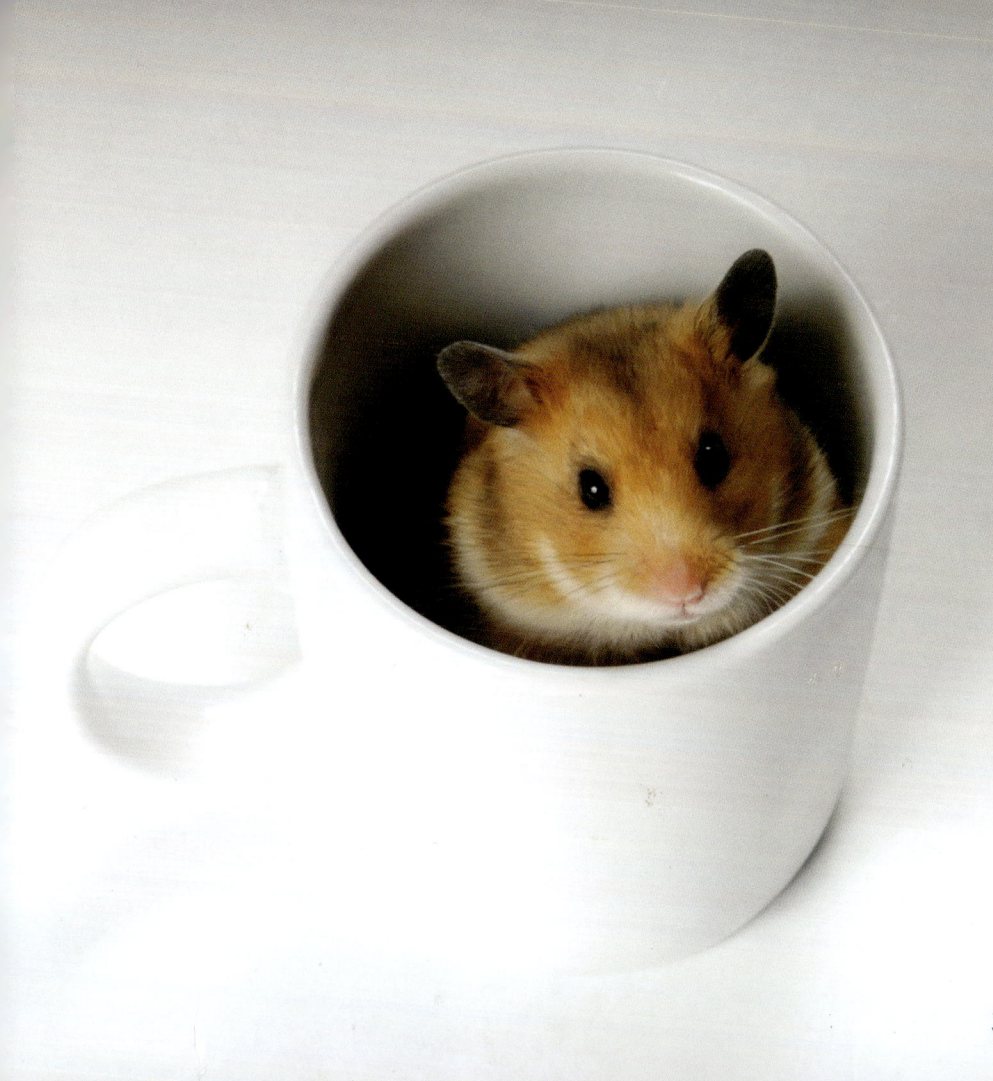

Look in the ball.

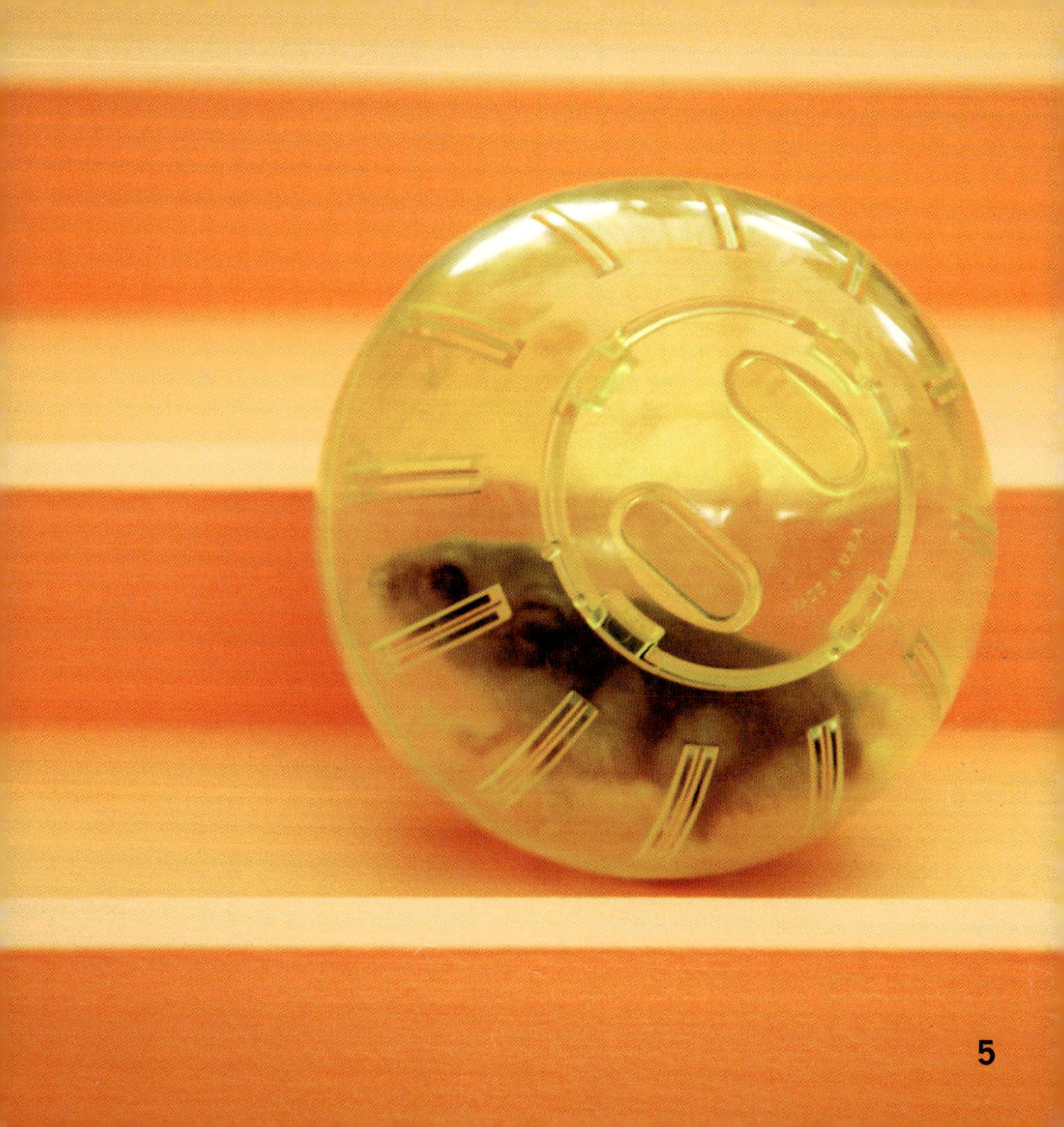

Look in the basket.

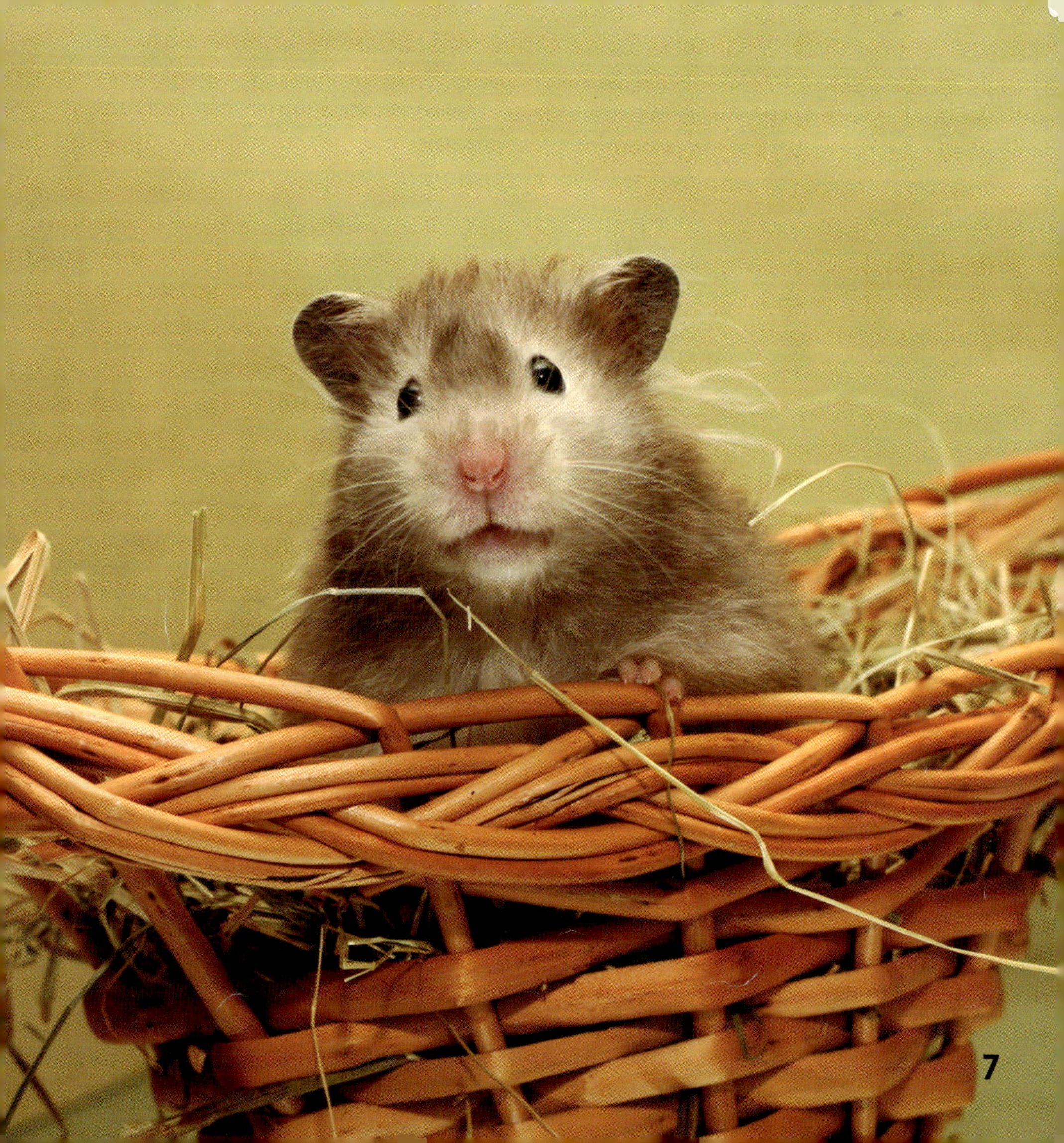

Look in the box.

9

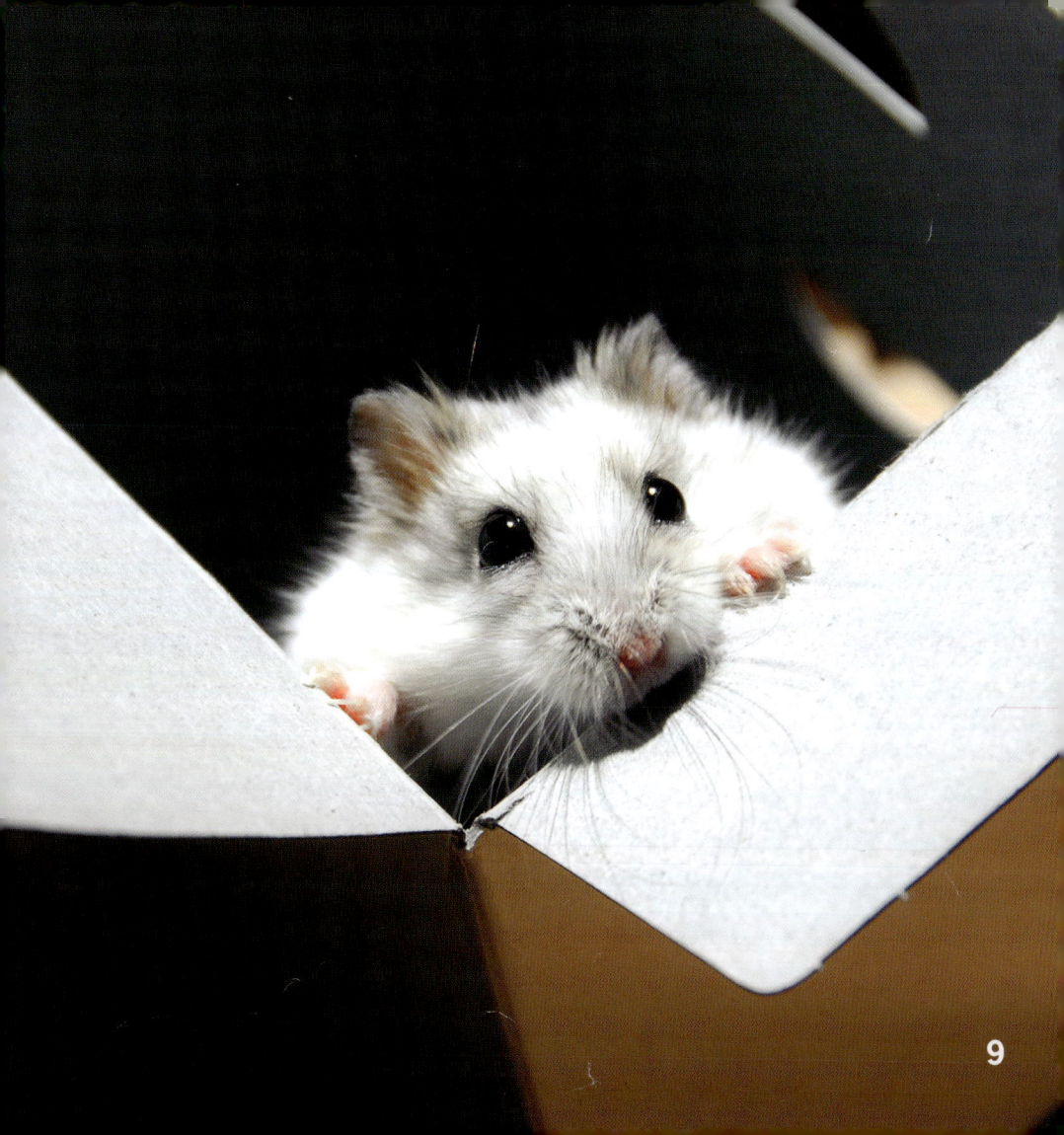

Look in the house.

11

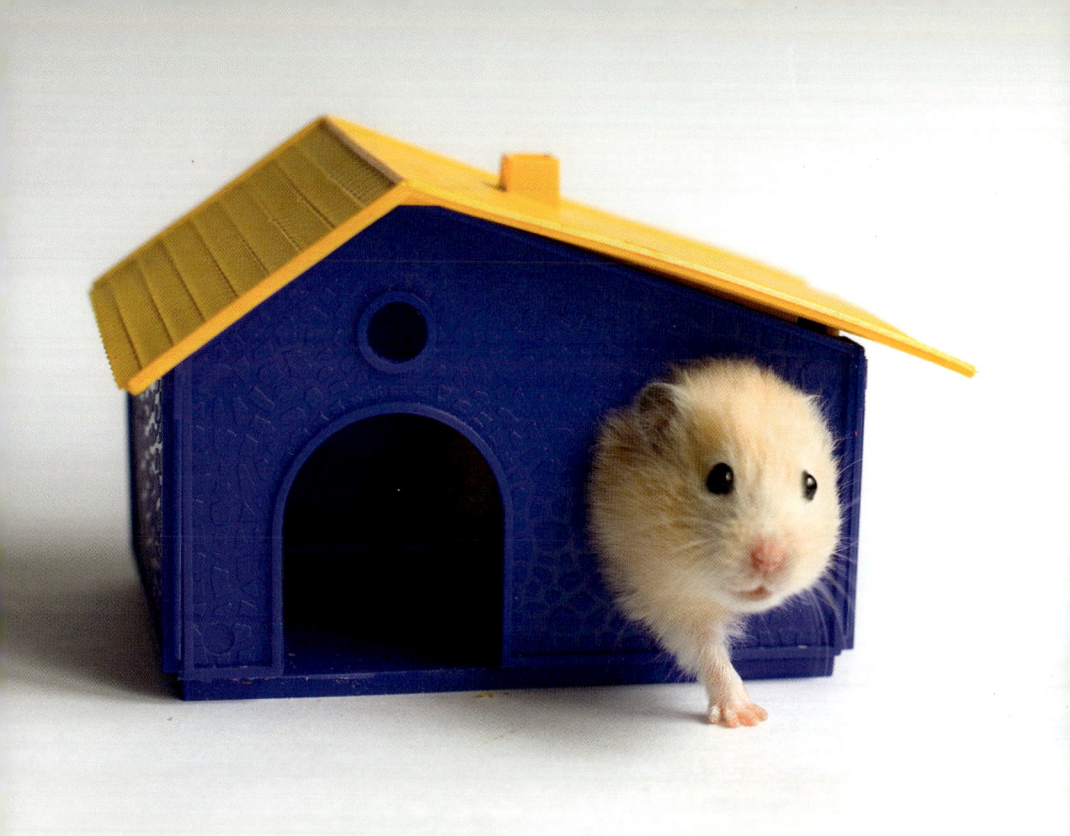

Look in my hand.

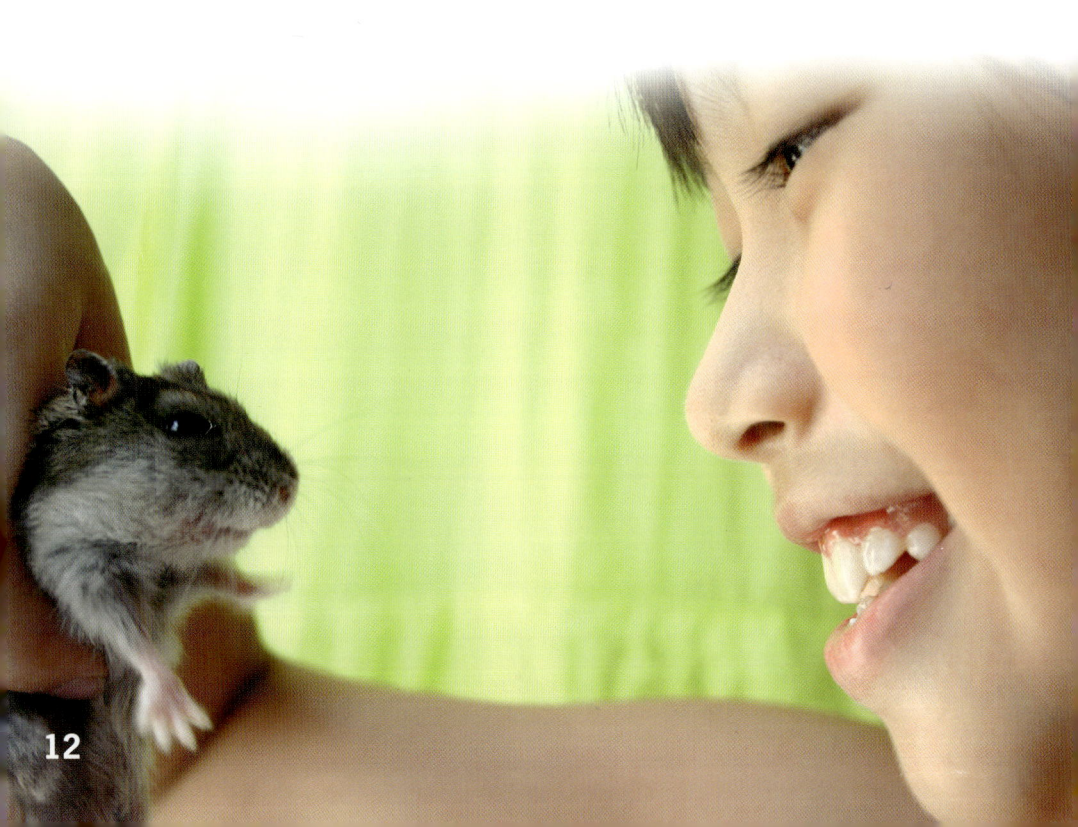